Wish for Spirit

Photographed and Written by:
Sarah Muehlbauer

Wish for Spirit

CONTENTS

artist

zeitgeist

rustic

epic

we should put in an extra stair / skylight

fallen roof / homogenic

the frame / shipwreck

wonderland / the hare

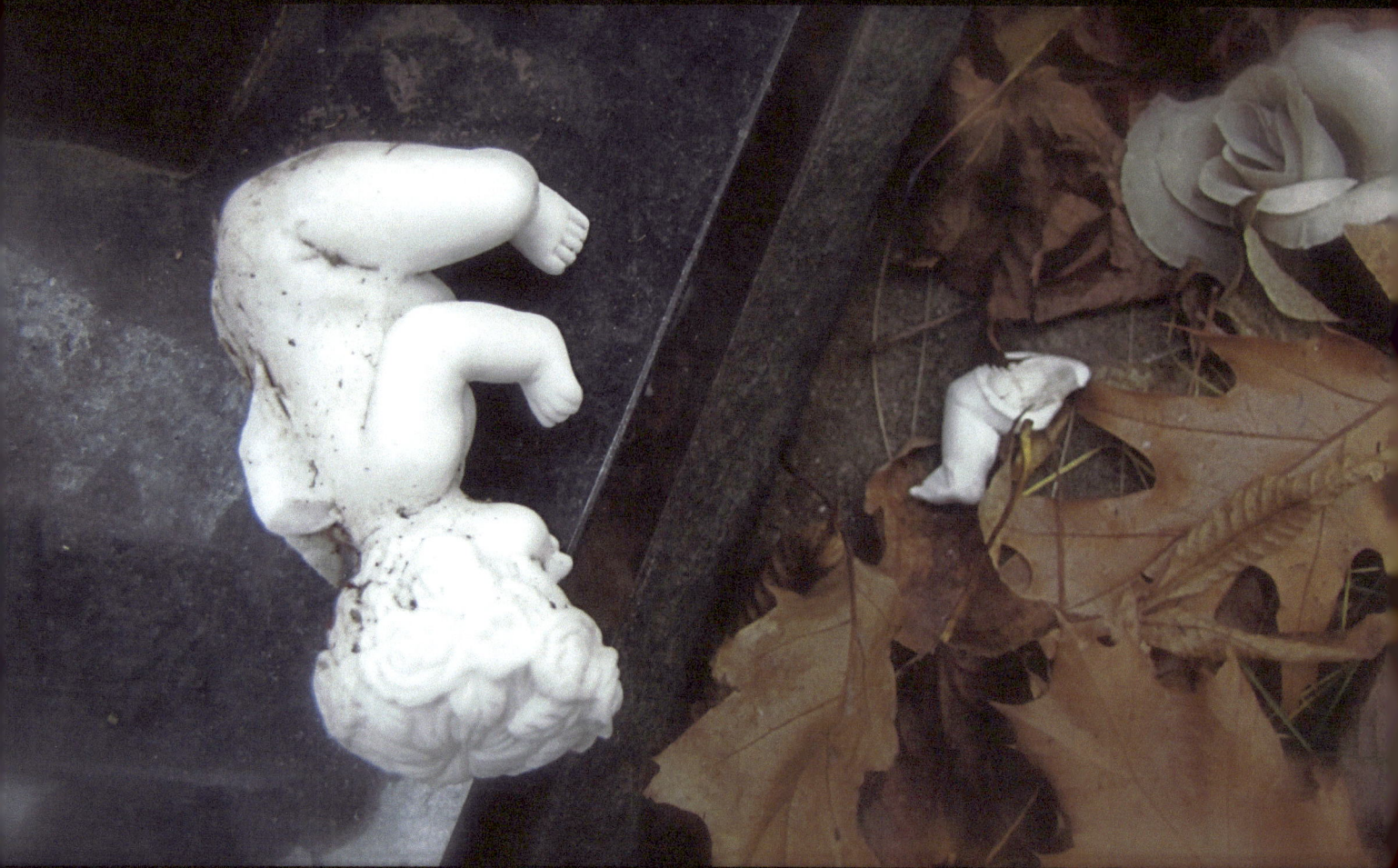

fallen limb / phoenix

Schlummere sanft guter Sohn.

KARL LISTEN.

JUNG

black virgin / white sun

e couleur

message in a bottle / embryo

addressing the foundations

Wish for Spirit

for my family

for everyone

www.ingramcontent.com/pod-product-compliance
Lightning Source LLC
Chambersburg PA
CBHW042006100426
42736CB00039B/208

* 9 7 8 0 6 9 2 2 0 9 3 7 0 *